W9-AVM-960

New Ideas for New Challenges

Wright Group

The **McGraw·Hill** Companies

www.WrightGroup.com

 **Wright Group**

Copyright © 2011 by The McGraw-Hill Companies, Inc.

Printed in China.

Send all inquiries to:
Wright Group/McGraw-Hill
P.O. Box 812960
Chicago, IL 60681

ISBN 978-0-07-656485-9
MHID 0-07-656485-1

1 2 3 4 5 6 7 8 9 DSS 15 14 13 12 11 10 09

Contents

Digital 21

My Home Page

ebook

online coach

How can new ideas change our lives and the world around us?

People are always coming up with new ideas. They look for ways to solve problems. They find new ways of doing things. They invent new things to use.

Mostly it takes a lot of work and determination to make an idea a reality. Sometimes new ideas create new challenges.

New ideas change how we live. They can make our lives safer, easier, and more fun. They can make our world a better place in which to live.

Focus Questions

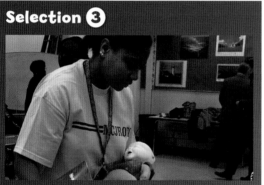

Preview ▶

online coach

How do inventions change life?
Preview pages 6–23. Then read
Strawberry City to find out.

Strawberry City

by Matthew Fisk

Illustrated by Richard Hoit

Chapter 1 Summer Vacation

"Bake corn bread," Dexter instructed the voice-activated oven. As the machine began humming, Dexter ate some more strawberries. Strawberries and corn bread were his favorite foods!

One of the best things about staying at Granddad's place was the food. Dexter was staying with him in Chicago for the summer vacation. It had rained nearly every day, and Dexter was glad the weather had finally improved.

"Corn bread baked," the oven announced to Dexter. It sounded a little like his teacher.

Dexter left the bread to cool and went to release Boris, his pet lizard, from his cage.

Dexter placed Boris gently near the strawberry bowl. "Another day in the big city, little friend," Dexter said.

Boris crept slowly alongside the bowl as his head swayed from side to side. Suddenly, as a fat fly buzzed lazily around the bowl, Boris stood still.

"Breakfast time," Dexter said.

In a flash Boris snatched the fly and gulped it.

announced: stated

7

"Mmm, that bread smells delicious," said Granddad, strolling into the kitchen. He switched on the Smart Pot. "Hey! Don't let Boris get the strawberries."

Dexter laughed. "He's **carnivorous**. He likes meat, not fruit."

Granddad poured his coffee. "So, any plans for today, Dexter?" he asked.

"Watch 3D-TV?"

"No. We need some **inspiration**."

Granddad picked up a strawberry and **rinsed** it. "You know where these come from, Dexter?"

"From that farm outside the city, of course. We went there the other day, Granddad."

"Yes, but before that?"

"From the ground, I guess."

Granddad grinned. "Not always, Dexter. Let's go strawberry picking!"

"But it's rush hour," Dexter said, puzzled. "It'll take hours to drive to the farm."

"Oh, I'm talking about a different farm, Dexter. Grab your jacket and let's go," said Granddad.

Dexter didn't think a farm trip sounded particularly interesting, so he decided to take Boris along. Secretly, he slipped the lizard into his jacket pocket.

Strategy Tool Kit
Make Predictions
What do you think will be different about the farm?

9

Chapter 2 Skyscraper Farms

Thirty minutes later they were outside a tall building in the heart of the city. "Park, please!" Granddad said, and the car steered itself perfectly into a parking space. "In my day we had to park the cars ourselves," laughed Granddad. "Imagine that!"

Dexter raised his eyebrows. "Weird."

"Welcome to Sky High Farm!" Granddad said as they entered the building.

"Wow! A farm in a skyscraper? Do they have tractors?" Dexter said.

"Let's find out."

The elevator zoomed up to the highest floor, where a woman dressed in green introduced herself.

"I'm Sonja, your guide," she said. "Your granddad told me that you like strawberries, Dexter."

"Yes! Do you **produce** any?" Dexter asked.

"Millions!" Sonja said.

Sonja **escorted** them into a huge room like a warehouse. Overhead, rows of fluorescent lights lit up the space. The black floor was laid out in long lines of large, leafy plants. As they wandered between the plants, Dexter looked at the floor. It appeared to be made from some type of plastic.

"Where's the soil?" Dexter asked.

"There isn't any," Sonja replied. "These strawberry plants are grown in water."

wandered: drifted

Dexter bent down and examined a plant. It was growing from a hole in the plastic, and he could see blue water flowing underneath the floor.

"Growing plants in water is called hydroponics," explained Sonja. "The water contains a special solution that has all the food a plant needs."

Dexter frowned. "But are the strawberries as good as the ones that grow in the ground?"

"Even better," grinned Sonja. "Growing plants without soil is a good way of finding out what nutrients plants really need to grow well. Hydroponics has cut down on pollution too. We don't need to use fancy fertilizers, which can cause pollution when they're produced."

"Isn't it expensive to grow plants inside?" asked Dexter.

"No, it's cheaper," Sonja said. "We can fit in more plants, and we don't need any digging machines. Plus, the weather is always fine!"

nutrients: food

Strategy Tool Kit
Ask and Answer Questions
What question would you have asked about hydroponics? What else have you learned about hydroponics from the text?

13

"How do you power all those lights?" Granddad asked.

"Solar energy," Sonja replied. "There's a layer of plastic that collects light on our rooftop. The plastic is built into the whole skyscraper too. It **gathers** up sunlight and turns it into electricity. Most businesses are doing the same thing now."

Granddad shook his head. "A long time ago people got their energy from fossil fuels. Factories had smoke pouring out of their chimneys! Back then, it was hard to imagine that one day the sun

would be powering almost every business."

Dexter put his hand in his pocket to check on Boris. The lizard was safely snuggled there.

"Try to find a strawberry," Sonja said.

Dexter lifted a leaf and found a bunch of the biggest strawberries he'd ever seen.

Stop and Think

How else might farming in the future be different from farming today?

Chapter 3 Pest Control

"Wow! Are they safe to eat?" he asked. "Have they been sprayed with pesticides?"

Sonja laughed. "They're very safe. We don't use poisonous chemicals."

"How do you control the pests then?" asked Granddad.

"We don't have pests inside the building," Sonja said. "That's another advantage of growing plants indoors—no swarms of insects!" Sonja walked away between the rows of plants. But Dexter hadn't finished examining the juicy-looking strawberries.

Dexter suddenly noticed the leaves beside him were moving. He froze. There was some kind of creature in the plants! Dexter saw two beady eyes staring at him through the leaves. Goosebumps rose on his skin. Was the creature friendly or not?

pesticides: bug sprays

Peering closer, Dexter realized it was a tiny machine. It was shaped like a pumpkin and had six arms that waved like feelers.

"So you've **discovered** our invention!" Sonja said as she came back.

"Yes," Dexter said. "What is it?"

"It's an MEM, or mini-electronic-machine. It picks up dead leaves that the strawberry plants have dropped and turns them into compost. Usually you have to wait a few weeks before compost is ready to use. But this machine makes instant compost! We sell the compost to gardeners."

The MEM hovered above a plant. It gently scooped up the dead leaves. The arms dropped the leaves into a hole on top of the MEM.

Suddenly the MEM plucked a strawberry and threw it high into the air. Dexter frowned. "Is it meant to do that?"

Sonja laughed. "It's not perfect yet! All inventions take time."

hovered: floated

Strategy Tool Kit
Ask and Answer Questions
What does Sonja mean by "All inventions take time"? How does this relate to what you've read elsewhere about inventions?

19

Chapter 4 Trying It at Home

Suddenly Dexter remembered Boris. He might have woken up. Dexter put his hand in his pocket. The lizard had <u>vanished</u>!

Dexter looked around. All he could see were endless rows of plants. How would he ever find his little friend Boris in this enormous place? Dexter **attempted** to find the plant where he'd bent over to pick the strawberry, but they all looked exactly the same. And what about the MEM? If it saw Boris, it might pick him up and throw him into the air. Worse, it might turn him into compost!

vanished: disappeared

"What's wrong, Dexter?" Granddad asked.

"I've lost Boris. Sorry, Granddad, I should have asked you if I could bring him," Dexter said.

"What is a Boris?" Sonja asked.

"My pet lizard."

"Oh, this lizard belongs to you? I found him sitting on a strawberry plant." Sonja opened her hand, and there was Boris.

Dexter took Boris from Sonja. "Thanks. I'll hold onto him."

Sonja showed them around the rest of Sky High Farm. On one level they saw corn plants growing so tall they touched the ceiling.

Sonja explained that nothing was wasted on the farm. Even the water and the air were cleaned and recycled for use again.

Finally it was time to leave.

"Thank you!" said Dexter. "That was even better than watching 3D-TV."

"Would you like to take a strawberry plant home?" Sonja asked.

"Sure! But how do I take care of it?"

"It's easy. I'll give you some growing **instructions**. I'm afraid I can't give you an MEM, though."

"That's OK. We've got a compost pile in the backyard." Dexter thought for a moment. "How will I control bugs?"

"You've got Boris!" Sonja said. "Lizards are excellent pest controllers."

Dexter laughed. Now he could grow his own strawberries to eat. And now Boris had something to keep him occupied too.

occupied: busy

23

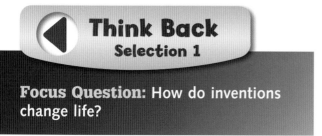

Focus Question: How do inventions change life?

A Check Understanding

How did an invention change the life of a character in *Strawberry City*? Write a paragraph about what life might be like for that character without the invention. PRACTICE COMPANION 293

B Understand Literary Elements ★★

Who is telling the story? Is it someone inside the story or outside? Explain to a partner what would happen with a different point of view.

C Share and Compare ★★

Choose an invention from the story. Draw a picture or diagram to show how it worked. Share it with a partner.

D Think Critically ★★★★

Discuss with your group how new ideas change our lives and the world around us. Use examples from your story to explain.

My Home Page

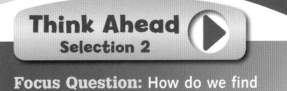

Focus Question: How do we find solutions?

Selection Connection

You have learned how inventions can change our lives. In the next selection you will learn more about how ideas change the world and how people find solutions.

★★★★
Show What You Know

How do you find a solution to a problem? With your group write a numbered list of the steps you take.

PRACTICE COMPANION **294**

Preview ▶

onl?ne coach

How do we find solutions?

Preview pages 26–45. Then read *Inventing to Solve Problems* to find out.

Inventing to Solve
Problems

by Regan Sparrow

fireworks

airplane

parachute

bubblegum

Chapter 1 Solving Problems

What do paper, pencils, parachutes, bicycles, bubblegum, and fireworks have in common? They are all inventions! Almost any human-made object you can name is someone's invention. At some time in the past, people found the inspiration to invent the objects around us today.

Some inventions were huge leaps in knowledge, such as the telephone, the car, and the airplane. They changed the lives of millions of people. But many other inventions concern little things in our everyday lives.

Most inventions, large or small, came about because people saw a problem that needed solving. Look around you. Is there anything you would like to change? If you were an inventor, what would your **ambition** be?

> concern: have to do with

To solve problems, inventors ask themselves questions. *How can I move that? Can I make this go faster? What if I put the wings here? If I change the shape of this, what will happen? Will adding water make a difference?* Anyone who asks these kinds of questions—and looks for the answers—can be an inventor.

seedpod

Lindsey Clement became an inventor when she was only eleven years old. Lindsey didn't like the messy seedpods the gum trees dropped all over her yard. So she invented a machine to pick up the spiky pods, or "gumballs." She tried many materials for her "gumball machine." Nothing worked well. Then she discovered that wire mesh snagged the seedpods. She was successful at last!

snagged: caught

Strategy Tool Kit
Monitor Comprehension
What problem did Lindsey Clement want to solve? Try explaining it.

Boring, **repetitive** work is a common problem that inspires some inventors. Having to do the same job over and over is tiresome. An inventor might ask, "How could I do this job more easily and quickly?"

Thomas Blanchard was one such inventor. He was born in 1788. As a child he liked to tinker with machines. When he was only thirteen, he invented a machine to peel apples. It made this boring job faster and easier.

This drawing shows another of Blanchard's inventions.

BLANCHARD'S.
Turning Machine.

Thomas Blanchard

Later Blanchard went to work in a tack factory. Making the tacks by hand was another tiresome job that took a long time. When he was eighteen, he invented a tack machine that took six years to finish. It is still used today, more than 200 years later.

MAKING COPIES

Part of Chester F. Carlson's job was copying drawings and other papers over and over by hand. Carlson wanted to invent a quick and simple way to make copies. It took him many years, but he succeeded in 1942 with his invention of the photocopier.

Carlson stands beside the first model of his copier.

Chapter 2 Thinking Creatively

Inventing something doesn't happen <u>instantly</u>. It is often a long process. An inventor must think of and try out many ideas before finding the one that works. Thinking creatively is the key to a successful invention.

Brainstorming is often the first step in thinking creatively. People can brainstorm either by themselves or in a group. They try to come up with as many ideas as possible to jump-start their thinking.

Being flexible and open to new ideas is another part of thinking creatively. Inventors can't get stuck on one idea. They need to be willing to change direction and try something new if their first ideas don't work.

instantly: right away

When people work in a group, they share their ideas.

Strategy Tool Kit
Summarize
In your own words, explain what is meant by brainstorming.

33

Sometimes thinking creatively means adding to existing ideas. Inventors might expand on someone else's invention and improve it in some way. Inventors can also improve their own inventions and make newer, better **versions**.

Thinking creatively also means being **original**. Inventors try to think of ideas no one has thought of before! This is often the hardest part.

expand: build

Over the years, improvements have been made to the telephone.

telephone

Even if an idea is new to you, someone else might have already thought of it. You can find out if an invention like yours already exists by doing a patent search at a library or online. A patent is a **document** given to inventors by the government. It grants only the inventor the right to make and sell his or her invention.

PATENT NUMBERS

A patented invention has a patent number on it somewhere. Patents usually take a lot of time and money to obtain, so you often find the words "Patent Pending" on a product. This means the inventor is waiting for the patent to be granted.

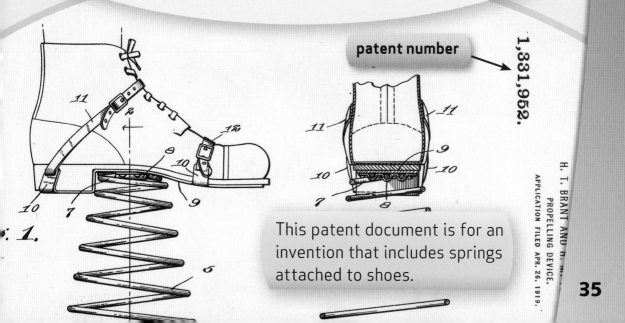

patent number

1,331,952.

H. T. BRANT AND ...
PROPELLING DEVICE.
APPLICATION FILED APR. 26, 1919.

This patent document is for an invention that includes springs attached to shoes.

In your classroom you use many inventions that came from creative thinking. The eraser, the pencil sharpener, the whiteboard—all of these inventions changed classrooms! One great classroom invention is the **crayon**. In the early 1900s children's crayons were made in Europe from charcoal and oil. They broke easily and were <u>expensive</u>.

expensive: costly

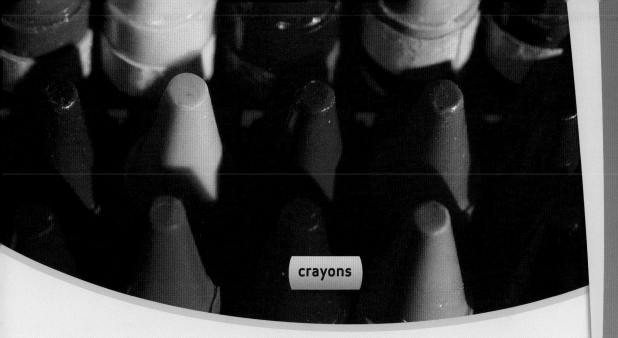

crayons

Americans Edwin Binney and Harold Smith began a company that made some of the colors that were used in paints and inks. When they saw the need for better crayons, they thought of a solution. They mixed their colors with wax. This made the crayons stronger and less expensive than the ones from Europe.

Binney and Smith's company still makes crayons today. It has sold more than 100 billion crayons to date!

Stop and Think

What inventions solve problems? How can inventors think creatively?

Chapter 3   Steps for Inventing

If you're going to be an inventor, you need to keep a
notebook! Write all your ideas in the notebook.
Include the date with each entry. Follow these steps:

notebook

1   **Define the problem.**

In one sentence write down the problem you are trying to solve.

2   **Collect information.**

Use sources such as an encyclopedia, library materials, and the Internet to find information about the problem. List important facts.

3   **Brainstorm possible solutions.**

Write down as many ideas as possible, no matter how silly.

4   **Narrow the choices.**

Choose the solution you think is the best.

5   **Draw it.**

Draw a picture of your solution. Add labels. List the supplies you will need to make your invention.

6   **Try it.**

You might need to try a few different models before you get it right. This is called trial and error. How do your mistakes help you improve your original idea?

Many inventors use notebooks for their ideas. The artist and inventor Leonardo da Vinci used notebooks to record his ideas for flying machines. He wrote backward from right to left. Some think this was to prevent people from stealing his ideas.

Leonardo da Vinci made very clear drawings of his ideas.

When inventors try to turn their ideas into reality, they can make mistakes. The inventor Otto Lilienthal had an idea to build a flying machine. As a teenager he built wings from wooden frames covered with linen. He strapped them on and ran down a hill flapping his arms. That didn't work! Soon Lilienthal tried building gliders. He made many more mistakes before he made the world's first successful flight in a glider in 1891. So don't worry if you make mistakes—you can learn from them.

Otto Lilienthal experiments with a glider in 1891.

Strategy Tool Kit
Monitor Comprehension
What was unusual about Leonardo da Vinci's notebooks?

Chapter 4 Keep Trying!

At every step of the process, inventors **revise**. They constantly take another look at their ideas to find the best solution. They might change a model many times to make it just right. They might have to run tests over and over again. Or they might need to take a totally new approach if their first—or second or third—idea does not work.

approach: method

This scientist is working on a new type of battery to store energy.

Sometimes other people can help an inventor see a problem in a new light. For this reason many inventors work in teams, either with a partner or as part of a larger group. Working together can spark new ideas, and team members can share the workload.

BLUE JEANS

In the mid-1850s, a storekeeper named Levi Strauss opened a dry goods store that sold supplies and cloth to miners. In 1872 a tailor told Strauss how he could use steel rivets to hold the seams of trousers together, making the trousers stronger. Strauss tried using brown cotton to make the trousers, but the cotton was stiff and uncomfortable. He found that denim was a better material because it became soft with wear. These changes turned the work trousers into the blue jeans that millions of people wear today.

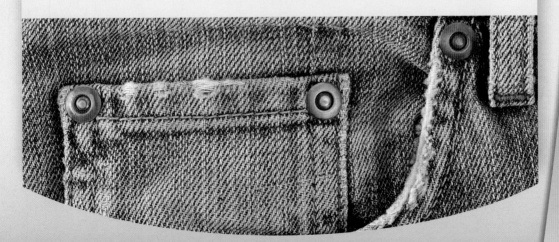

Working in teams can be a challenge too. Team members must agree on what to work on and how to approach a task. Everyone must do his or her share of the work. Teamwork requires **cooperation** with others and respect for their ideas.

These students are working together to build a model out of straws and clay.

straw

clay

Sum It Up

However you choose to work—in a team or on your own—you must keep your goal in sight. Remember what you are working toward and why. Most inventors will tell you that solving a problem takes a lot of time and effort. You must have a great deal of patience and persistence. But inventors will also tell you that the rewards of making a successful invention are worth it!

persistence: will power

Think Back
Selection 2

Focus Question: How do we find solutions?

A ## Check Understanding ★

Working to Solve a Problem gave some ideas about how to find a solution to a problem. List the main ideas suggested. `PRACTICE COMPANION` **310**

B ## Understand Text Features ★★

Look up some highlighted words from your selection in the Glossary to see their meanings and how they are pronounced. With a partner, say the words and use them in sentences.

C ## Share and Compare ★★

Choose a problem and solution from your selection. Make a T chart with your partner that tells about the problem and gives the solution.

D ## Think Critically ★★★★

Discuss with your group how new ideas change our lives and the world around us. Use examples from your selection to explain.

My Home Page

Think Ahead
Selection 3

Focus Question: How can learning
something new change our lives?

Selection Connection

You have read about how people have tried new
ideas that changed the world. Now read about
how learning something new might change
your life.

★★★★
Show What You Know

Discuss with your group
something you have learned
that has made a difference to
your life. How did your life
change? PRACTICE COMPANION **311**

Preview ▶ online coach

**How can learning something
new change our lives?** Preview
pages 48–65. Then read *Beyond
the Comfort Zone* to find out.

Beyond the Comfort Zone

by Eve Tonkin

Illustrated by Marsela Hajdinjak-Krec

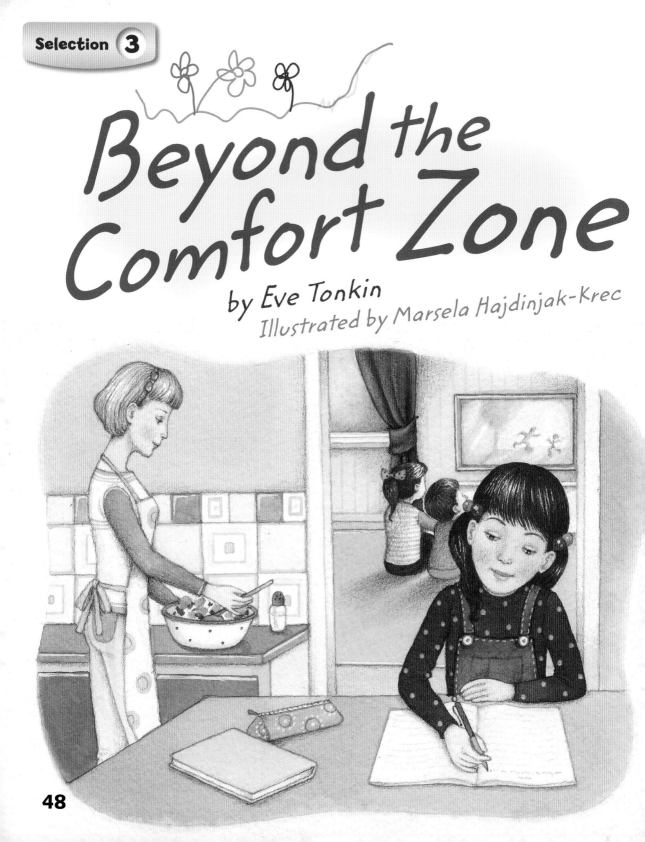

October 15

Dear Diary,

Sarah here. I've just finished my homework, and I'm writing this while Hannah and Joel watch TV. Nancy is fixing a salad for dinner. Mom and Dad are both working late at the hospital again. They pinned a photograph of themselves to the refrigerator door—Mom is sticking out her tongue, and Dad is doing his monkey face. Underneath it says "Crazy About Seeing You Tomorrow."

October 16

Guess what? This morning at breakfast Mom said she and Dad have something <u>urgent</u> to talk to us about. We're going to have a family conference after dinner. I hope we're going somewhere exciting on vacation.

Mom had us try a new cereal. She says it is **healthier** than the old one. (That's the problem with having doctors for parents!) Joel and I pretended we were advertising it on TV, and Hannah accidentally tipped hers out on the floor.

urgent: important

The family conference wasn't about a vacation. Mom and Dad explained that they want us to spend more time together as a family, so they've **resigned** from their jobs. They've got new part-time jobs a long way away, in a small community in the mountains. We're going to move before Hanukkah arrives.

We won't celebrate this year with our grandparents, Bubby and Zaidy, or with Uncle Jay and Aunt Anna. We'll be leaving our caregiver, Nancy, behind too. But Mom and Dad promise to be at home more often. I'll still miss everyone.

Hannah and I were sad about saying good-bye to our friends. Joel cried about leaving our home and going somewhere strange. Mom, Dad, and Nancy hugged us. When we felt better, Dad said that what we were feeling was a normal part of going "beyond the comfort zone."

"When you do something new, you sometimes feel upset or scared because it seems **risky** or uncomfortable," Dad explained. "But imagine if you kids had never tried going beyond your comfort zones—you wouldn't have learned to walk!"

Dad suggested that I make a list of the good things about going beyond the comfort zone when a person moves to a new place. We came up with the first two things together:

Going Beyond the Comfort Zone

1. We'll live in a house instead of an apartment.
2. We'll have space for a dog.

December 8

The moving vans came today. They took away all our belongings. It felt weird looking at our empty apartment. We're going to stay with Bubby and Zaidy for a week, and then we're leaving.

December 13

It's fun at Bubby and Zaidy's. Zaidy sneaks us treats when Bubby and Mom are out of the room. (I think they know about it, though!)

Strategy Tool Kit
Visualize
Picture what it looked and felt like for Sarah as she stood in the empty apartment.

December 15

We're leaving tomorrow. Everyone came over for dinner last night to say **farewell** to us. Bubby kept hugging us. Zaidy and I cried. Then today we said good-bye to Nancy. I don't want to move!

December 19

We've been driving for three days! At first it was sad and boring, but then we started to have fun. Mom started us off playing games, and we held a joke contest. (Dad's jokes were the worst, so he won.)

We've been to some great places, like a pioneer village and a motel with a pool shaped like a snake. We're in the mountains now, and it's really beautiful. You can see a lake through the tall pines. A deer just peered at us! Dad says now it's not far to our new home. I'm looking forward to seeing it.

Going Beyond the Comfort Zone

3. We'll experience new things.

Stop and Think

What are some examples of times that you have gone beyond your comfort zone?

Our new house is so cool! It's way better than our apartment in the city. All the bedrooms are on the second floor. My room looks out on the woods. Dad is going to help me hang up a bird feeder. I'm glad we moved, although I still miss everyone.

We lit the first Hanukkah candle tonight. We felt sad thinking of Bubby and Zaidy. During our meal the windowpanes started to rattle. Hail **spattered** on the ground, the wind screeched, and now it's snowing! I've never seen snow before. We're going to make a snowman in the morning.

No snowman today—it's still snowing! All I can see outside is a **whirling** white mass. No TV because the electricity is out. Everything is in a mess and there's nothing to do except unpack. I can't think of anything to add to my list today.

December 22

Last night was the best fun *ever*! Dad asked Joel and me to help drag in loads of firewood, and we built a huge fire and cooked on it. It was great. Afterward Dad and I played checkers. We've never done that after dinner before—we would just watch TV or play video games.

The nicest part was lighting the candles and putting the menorah beside the window to shine out into the snow.

December 23

The snow has stopped, but the electricity is still out—hooray! After Dad helped us make toast over the fire, we raced straight outside. We made a huge snowman. Dad started digging snow from our driveway.

Going Beyond the Comfort Zone

3. We'll experience new things.
LIKE SNOW! AND NO ELECTRICITY!

Strategy Tool Kit
Visualize
Imagine the landscape, the sounds, and how the children felt as they built their first snowman.

We heard a noisy engine in the distance, and Dad said it was the snowplow clearing the roads. Mom went inside to get a shovel to help Dad clear the snow. Then a truck stopped at our mailbox. A family **clambered** over the snowdrifts, carrying shovels. They started digging snow out of our driveway. Joel and I ran to help, and we met the new family halfway. There was a boy and a girl about the same age as Joel and me.

"Hi there!" said the father. "I'm Tom Wilson!"

"Mr. Wilson is in charge of the medical center where we'll be working," Dad explained to us.

"We thought you might be snowed in without anything warm to eat," said Mr. Wilson, "so we brought some soup to share with you. This is my wife, Samantha, and our children, Clara and Antonio."

Mrs. Wilson smiled at us. "We really **appreciate** our doctors up here in the mountains," she said, "so having two of you is a real advantage."

advantage: edge

We all went inside to thaw out and have lunch. Joel, Hannah, and I played with Clara and Antonio all afternoon. After awhile Clara and I went up to my room. She's really cool. My books were all **jumbled** up, so she helped me shelve them.

"Do you like ice-skating?" Clara asked me.

"I've never tried it," I said. I was worried that Clara might think it was uncool to have never tried ice-skating. But she looked really excited.

"I'll teach you!" she said.

We made a plan to go ice-skating next week. I can't wait! I just hope I don't fall over too often.

Before she went, Clara wrote a welcome note in my diary. Then she drew a picture of herself.

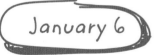

January 6

School starts tomorrow. I'll be in the same class as Clara, so I don't feel **anxious** (well, maybe I do, but only a little bit!).

Strategy Tool Kit
Summarize
What has led the girls to becoming friends?

January 9

It's great being at a small school. It's easy to get to know everyone. My teacher, Mrs. Mickelson, is nice. She <u>knitted</u> her scarf. It's so long it wraps around her neck twice.

Mrs. Mickelson asked us to write a poem about our winter break. She said it could be about something we did or something we learned. At first I didn't know what to write. I've been doing so many different things. Then I realized I could write about them all!

knitted: made

Here's what I wrote:

Beyond the Comfort Zone

We left empty rooms behind,
said good-bye to Zaidy and his cookies,
Bubby and her hugs, as warm
as a house in winter.
As we drove away
I kept wishing it were all a dream
and that I would open my eyes and find myself home.
Then we saw life in the mountains.
Welcoming rooms were waiting for us,
and in the soft snow heaped on the ground,
snowmen were waiting to be made.
We lit the candles for a new year.

Think Back
Selection 3

Focus Question: How can learning something new change our lives?

A **Check Understanding** ★

How did learning something new change the life of a character in *Beyond the Comfort Zone*? Imagine you are the character and write an e-mail to a friend that explains. PRACTICE COMPANION **339**

B **Understand Literary Elements** ★★

What problem did a character face in the selection? Explain to a partner how the problem was solved.

C **Share and Compare** ★★

List the things you admire about a character in your story. Compare your list with a partner's list.

D **Think Critically** ★★★★

Discuss with your group how new ideas change our lives and the world around us. Use examples from your selection to explain.

My Home Page

Selection Connection

You have learned that new ideas can change our lives and affect the world. Now read how inventions can also create challenges.

★★★★

Show What You Know

Brainstorm with your group an idea or invention that has good and bad things about it. Draw two columns with the headings "Benefits" and "Challenges" and write down what these are.

PRACTICE COMPANION 340

Preview ▶

online coach

How might inventions create a new challenges?

Preview pages 68–88. Then read *Science Meets Fiction* to find out.

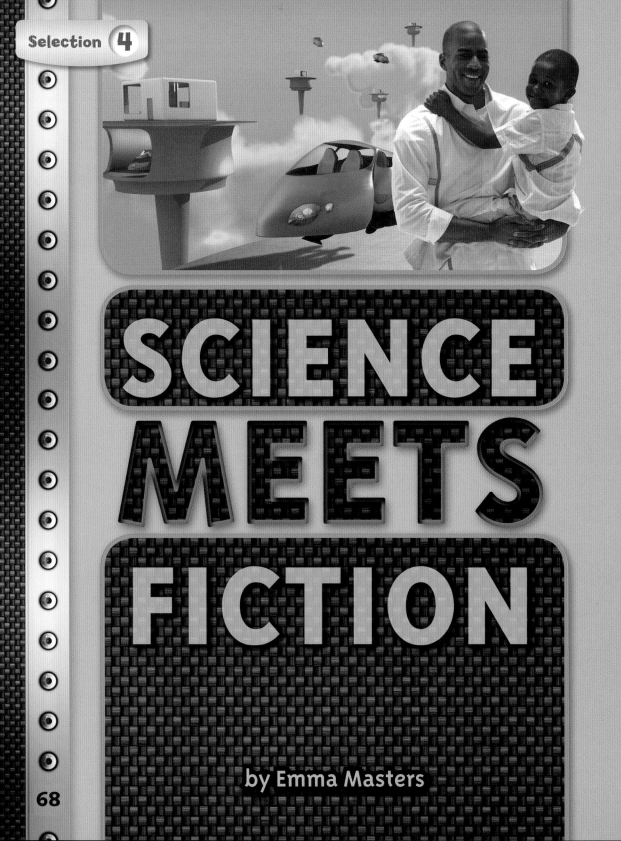

SCIENCE MEETS FICTION

by Emma Masters

CHAPTER 1
Our New Future

Exciting things are being invented every day. Many of these inventions will have great **benefits**. They will save time and make our lives easier. Some inventions might be able to do those chores for us. Then people would have more time to work or relax.

Scientists solve problems and overcome challenges when they invent. Scientists also test inventions to make sure they work properly.

Read on to find out about some inventions that could change our lives.

These designers are looking at a new car design on large-screen monitors.

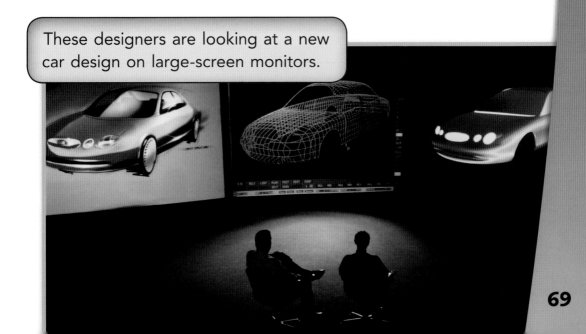

Keeping Up with Technology

People are always improving inventions. Technology keeps changing. Computers and TVs now can use the same screen. We can buy special receiver boxes. These let us watch Internet movies on a TV set.

Scientists are testing a remote control that has only one button. This one-button remote control will operate TVs, lights, and game consoles. So how would it work? You would point the remote control at a screen. From that screen you would select the item that you want to control.

remote control

Who knows how technology might change the way we listen to music?

Our clothing might also be able to do new things in the future. It might charge our cell phones or MP3 players. We might be able to change its color **according to** our mood. One inventor has designed a shirt that can make music. The wearer simply moves his or her arms as if playing a guitar. A computer then turns the movements into musical sounds!

Strategy Tool Kit
Make Connections
What technology do you use at home and at school?

Modern cell phones can be a lot of fun to use.

The Small Stuff

The first cell phones were used only to make and receive calls. Today we can store music and photos on cell phones. We can use them to watch movies and connect to the Internet. In the future cell phones will be able to do much more. People might use cell phones to control their homes. They could adjust the temperature or security system. People might even pay for items or plan meals on their phones!

adjust: change

Cell phones are getting smaller and smaller.

Something so small can be easy to lose, however. This would be like losing a wallet, keys, MP3 player, and cell phone all at once! Scientists are developing ways to help people find their lost cell phones easily.

CHAPTER 2
Smart Homes

Homes with lots of technology are called smart homes. People in these homes can unlock their doors while pulling into their driveways. They can turn on the lights before walking through the door. They can clap their hands to switch on music.

This screen is part of this smart home's control system.

What would it be like to live in a smart home of the future? Your house will wake you up each morning. It will remind you to take your gym clothes to school. It will turn on your shower to the right temperature. It will turn on lights when you walk into a room. Our homes will know our **routine**. They will have things <u>prepared</u> for our return.

prepared: ready

Smart houses would change the way we live.

In a smart home a computer would make all the appliances work together. For example, imagine you are leaving your house. Turning on a security alarm would **automatically** switch off the lights and adjust heating or air-conditioning. This technology will be **wireless**. A push of a button will control everything!

Smart homes might also be safer. In an emergency the smart home would wake you with an alarm. It would unlock doors and dial an emergency service. Then it would light a path to safety.

This man is using a computer to control the light in his home.

Using computers to control our homes might create problems, however. Will the smart home still work in a power outage? What if a computer virus ruins the smart home's programming? What if a smart home is just too confusing to use? The challenge for scientists is to solve these problems.

BRIGHT LIGHTS

Scientists have invented a new lighting system that is a thin sheet that can fit into surfaces like walls, tabletops, and ceilings. It has twice the efficiency and 10 times the lifetime of a regular lightbulb. It is not available yet because scientists are still experimenting with this idea.

Stop and Think
How would the new technology in Chapters 1 and 2 make a difference in your life?

CHAPTER 3
Robots

What do you imagine when you think about the future? Perhaps you imagine jet packs, time travel machines, and robots! Robots are already doing many jobs in our world today. Robots often carry out programmed instructions. They do tasks that are too dangerous or difficult for people. Robots are sent deep underground, to war zones, and even to other planets.

Scientists are working on a new type of robot that might be able to do other jobs such as nursing. These robots will be able to tell how people are feeling. They will have a built-in camera that will watch a patient's face. They will listen to the patient's voice. These robots will be able to speak and understand thousands of words.

robot

scientist

This scientist is demonstrating a robot that looks a lot like a human.

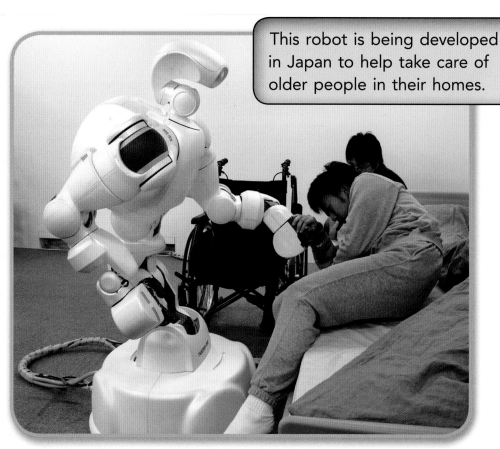

This robot is being developed in Japan to help take care of older people in their homes.

Here to Help

In the future robots might help us with more of our chores at home. We might have robots that make beds, do laundry, and put away dishes.

One problem with robots is movement. How will they move around our homes? Robots need to know when objects are in their way. Inventors are trying to make robots that can **sense** where objects are. Then the robots can move carefully around them.

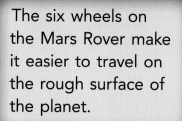

The six wheels on the Mars Rover make it easier to travel on the rough surface of the planet.

Inventors have also discovered that robots with two legs can be clumsy. They have studied how insects move. Inventors know that six legs work better on hills and bumps. Six-legged robots are now used in uneven places, such as the ocean floor. Maybe one day six-legged robots will work around the house too.

Strategy Tool Kit
Summarize
What are good things about robots? What are the main problems?

CHAPTER 4
Doing More with Less

Robots and other inventions might not always be made from the natural resources we use today. Fossil fuels, minerals, and wood might be scarce or very expensive in the future. People have to keep this in mind when inventing something new.

scarce: rare

Some scientists worry that new technologies might drain natural resources.

copper mine

In Abu Dhabi, United Arab Emirates, people are planning to build an "eco city" that will use very few natural resources.

In the meantime, scientists are investigating many ideas to help people and cities use fewer natural resources. They are testing new kinds of materials for building houses. They are trying to design systems that use less water and energy to cool and heat buildings. Other scientists are looking at ways to reduce and recycle waste. These new ideas might change the way we live and work.

 ## Sustainable Living

Inventors are not always thinking about the next new gadget! They also think about how people can live in **sustainable** ways. This means living in a way that is kind to the environment. It means taking care of Earth's natural resources. Then we will have enough in the future.

This building in San Bruno, California, has a green roof and solar panels.

One idea for sustainable living already exists in many cities. It's called green roofing. People plant grass on the rooftop of a building. This saves energy. The green roof cools the building in summer and heats it in winter. The grass also absorbs air pollutants. It soaks up a lot of storm water and reduces floods.

absorbs: soaks up

This house uses energy from the sun and recycles water.

Some houses are designed to use very few **nonrenewable** resources. These sustainable houses might be powered by energy from the sun or wind. They might use less water. They might make less waste and pollution. Today sustainable homes are expensive to build and operate. But people are finding ways to make these houses less costly.

A LIVING TREE HOUSE

Can you imagine growing a house from a living tree? A group of scientists is trying to do just that. Builders would use an ancient gardening method to weave tree branches together. The house would take shape over many years. This kind of idea seems strange today. But one day in the future, it could be a reality.

Solar Panels

Scientists are already designing cities that will run on solar power. But solar panels are expensive. A lot of energy is used to make them. One possible solution is a special dye that coats windows. The dye traps energy from the sun. It sends the energy to a solar cell to make electricity. Scientists are working on a way to make the dye last longer than a few months.

solar panels

Strategy Tool Kit
Make Connections
Have you seen solar panels or other images of them? Where were the solar panels?

Technology is a work that is always in progress. New inventions can make our lives easier and more enjoyable. But they often create challenges. We need to keep our eyes open. Then we will find ways to overcome the problems. Our world is always changing. Our ideas are always changing too.

progress: change

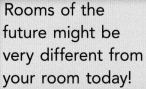

Think Back
Selection 4

Focus Question: How might inventions create new challenges?

A Check Understanding ★

How did an invention or a new idea in *Science Meets Fiction* create new challenges? List those challenges. PRACTICE COMPANION 359

B Understand Text Features ★★

Choose the most interesting sidebar in your selection. What new information did you learn? Share it with a partner.

C Share and Compare ★★

Discuss with a partner how a challenge from your selection might be overcome. Summarize your ideas for a partner.

D Think Critically ★★★★

Discuss with your group how new ideas change our lives and the world around us. Use examples from your selection to explain.

My Home Page

How can new ideas change our lives and the world around us?

Use these activities to show what you've learned about the theme question.

Design and Create

1. With a partner create a poster advertising an invention from the past or one that you think might be invented in the future.

2. Include a picture of the invention.

3. Add some text to persuade people to buy or use the invention.

4. Include information about any challenges of the invention.

Take the Stage

1. Choose an idea that has changed people's lives.

2. Create a play showing the events leading up to the moment when the inventor made his or her discovery.

3. Present your play to the class.

Book Club

1. Write three questions that you would like answered about a new idea or invention that was mentioned in your selections.

2. Use books, the library, or the Internet to find the answers to your questions.

3. Write a sentence or paragraph to answer each question.

Be an Author

1. Choose an invention or idea that has benefits and challenges.

2. List the good and bad things about the invention or idea in note form.

3. Write a persuasive article, explaining why we should make use of the invention or idea or why it should be controlled or banned.

Glossary

Pronunciation Key

a	bat	oi	toy
ā	ape	ou	shout
air	air	ŏŏ	book
ä	park	ōō	moon
e	let	s	sun
ē	easy	sh	pressure
i	if	th	the, thing
ī	lie	u	nut
îr	dear	ûr	circle
k	cause	ə	ago
o	lot	ər	mother
ō	go	′	primary stress
ô	all	′	secondary stress

according to (ə kôr′ ding tōō) *prep.* depending on;
The lizard could change color according to its surroundings. **71**

ambition (am bish′ ən) *n.* the drive to achieve;
My ambition is to become a doctor. **27**

anxious (angk′ shəs) *adj.* uneasy or worried;
Marta has an anxious look on her face. **63**

appreciate (ə prē′ shē āt) *v.* to be thankful for something;
The team did appreciate all the help their coach had given them. **61**

attempt (ə tempt′) *v.* to try;
Her goal was to attempt the marathon. **20**

automatically (ô tə mat′ ik lē) *adv.* done without a person controlling;
The lights in the house went on automatically when someone came in the door. **76**

benefit (ben′ ə fit) *n.* a good outcome;
The benefit of using coupons is saving money. **69**

carnivorous (kär niv′ ər əs) *adj.* feeding on meat;
Some types of lizards are carnivorous. **8**

clamber (klam′ bər) *v.* to climb awkwardly over something;
They had to clamber over the fence to get to the park. **60**

cooperation (kō op′ ə rā′ shən) *n.* the act of working together on a task; They got the job finished more quickly through cooperation. **44**

crayon (krā′ on) *n.* a stick of colored wax for writing or drawing; I used a purple crayon for the poster. **36**

discover (di skuv′ ər) *v.* to find out; Scientists may discover new planets. **18**

document (dok′ yə mənt) *n.* a piece of writing, usually on paper; The inventor obtained a patent document for his invention. **35**

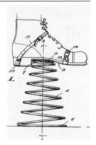

escort (es kôrt′) *v.* to take someone to a place; I will escort you to the gate if you don't know the way. **11**

farewell (fair wel′) *n.* a good-bye; Their teacher said farewell to all the students on the last day of school. **54**

gather (gath′ ər) *v.* to collect things together; They went to the store to gather the food for the picnic. **14**

healthier (hel′ thē ər) *adj.* better for someone's health; Fruit is a healthier snack than fries. **49**

inspiration (in′ spə rā′ shən) *n.* a sudden and exciting idea; Inventors may get an idea in a moment of inspiration. **9**

instruction (in struk′ shən) *n.* a thing that tells a person how to do something; He read the instruction for how to paint his bike. **23**

jumble (jum′ bəl) *v.* to mix up; The dryer will jumble the clothes. **62**

nonrenewable (non′ ri nōō′ ə bəl) *adj.* not easily replaced; Copper is a nonrenewable resource. **86**

original (ə rij′ ə nəl) *adj.* something that is completely new; His original idea was making a car that ran on water. **34**

produce (prə dōōs′) *v.* to make; Bees produce honey in the hive. **11**

repetitive (ri pet′ i tiv) *adj.* the act of doing something over and over; Peeling the potatoes for the camp was boring and repetitive. **30**

resign (ri zīn′) *v.* to leave your job; She decided to resign and move to the city. **50**

revise (ri vīz′) *v.* to go over something to try to make it better; He always tried to revise his essays before handing them in. **42**

rinse (rins) *v.* to wash something under water; He went to rinse the apple before he ate it. **9**

risky (ris′ kē) *adj.* full of danger; It is risky to greet a strange dog. **52**

routine (rōō tēn′) *n.* a set of things that are done at similar times; Part of his routine was to go for a run before school. **75**

sense (sens) *v.* to tell by using senses like touching or seeing; The dog barked when it could sense there was someone at the door. **80**

spatter (spat′ ər) *v.* to splash heavily; The rain began to spatter on the window as the storm started. **56**

sustainable (sə stā′ nə bəl) *adj.* continuing for a long time; Solar power is sustainable because it doesn't use up natural resources. **84**

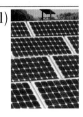

version (vûr′ zhən) *n.* a form of an original; The band recorded a different version of the song. **34**

whirling (hwûrl′ ing) *adj.* spinning and going in all directions; They found it hard to drive through the whirling snowstorm. **57**

wireless (wīr′ lis) *adj.* working without being connected with a wire; He could use his wireless computer outside. **76**

Index

Acknowledgments

Art Credits: ©The McGraw-Hill Companies, Inc. would like to thank the following illustrators for their contributions: Richard Hoit and Marsela Hajdinjak-Krec.

Photo Credits: 4 ©Tim Platt/Getty Images; **5** (tl) ©Stockbyte/PunchStock; (tr) ©Collections of Pattern Lumbermen's Museum, Courtesy of www.MaineMemory.net; (bl) ©Associated Press; (br) ©Stockxpert Images/Jupiterimages; **25** (l) ©Brand X Pictures/PunchStock; (c) ©Alexander Walter/ Getty Images; (r) ©Elizabeth Dunnack; **26** (tl) ©Eyewire (Photodisc)/PunchStock; (tr) ©Royalty-Free/Corbis; (bl) ©Jayme Thornton/Getty Images; (br) ©Photos.com/Jupiterimages; **28** ©Ryan McVay/Getty Images; **29** ©Dani Carlo/age Fotostock; **30** ©The Granger Collection, New York; (inset) courtesy of National Part Service; **31** ©Bettmann/Corbis; **33** ©Tim Platt/Getty Images; **34** (l) ©PhotoObjects.net/ Jupiterimages; (r) ©AbleStock.com/Jupiterimages; **35** ©MJ Rivise Patent Collection/Getty Images; **36** ©Jose Luis Pelaez Inc/Getty Images; **37** ©Comstock Images/Jupiterimages; **38** ©David Fischer/Getty Images; **40** ©Alinari Archives/Corbis; **41** ©Bettmann/Corbis; **42** ©Christian Science Monitor/Getty Images; **43** ©Stockxpert/Jupiterimages; **44** ©Michael Newman/PhotoEdit; **45** ©LWA-Sharie Kennedy/ Corbis; **46** ©Comstock Images/Jupiterimages; **47** (l) ©Paul Costello/Getty Images; (c) ©Jupiterimages/ Getty Images; (r) ©Jupiterimages/Getty Images; **67** (l) ©Thinkstock Images/Jupiterimages; (r) ©Koichi Kamoshida/Getty Images; **68–88** ©Stockxpert/Jupiterimages; **68** ©Jayme Thornton/Getty Images; **69** ©Louie Psihoyos/Science Faction/Corbis; **70** ©Corbis/Photolibrary; **71** ©Jose Luis Pelaez, Inc./ Corbis; **72** ©Ronnie Kaufman/Getty Images; **73** ©Thomas Northcut/Getty Images; **74** ©Richard Wadey/Alamy; **75** ©Ted Soqui/Corbis; **76** ©AFP/Getty Images; **77** ©ERproductions Ltd/Getty Images; **78** ©JPL-Caltech/NASA/Corbis; **79** ©Getty Images; **80** ©Associated Press; **81** ©NASA; **82** ©Photodisc/ Getty Images; **83** ©Stockxpert/Jupiterimages; **84** ©Comstock Images/Alamy; **85** ©Proehl Studios/ Corbis; **86** ©Brand X Pictures/Jupiterimages; **87** ©Stockxpert/Jupiterimages; **88** ©Jayme Thornton/ Getty Images; **89** ©Stockxpert/Jupiterimages; **93** ©Stockxpert/Jupiterimages.